'Belvidere Racket Ground'. This engraving first appeared in 1858 and shows an early form of rackets played outdoors against one wall.

TENNIS, SQUASH AND BADMINTON BYGONES

Gerald N. Gurney

Shire Publications Ltd

CONTENTS

Set in 9 point Times and printed in Great Britain by C. I. Thomas & Sons (Haverfordwest) Ltd, Press Buildings, Merlins Bridge, Haverfordwest, Dyfed SA61 1XE.

TO JOAN AND ANSELM

ACKNOWLEDGEMENTS

My largest debt is to Valerie Warren, Assistant Curator, the Wimbledon Lawn Tennis Museum, for her keen interest and advice as well as for the most generous provision of photographs. Other photographs were taken by Grandad's Photography Museum, Colchester; some of these have previously appeared in the Antique Collectors' Club *Journal*. Information has been generously given by Bow Brand Limited, Grays of Cambridge Limited, Slazengers Limited and the Dunlop Sports Company Limited, as well as by John Jaques Limited, specialists in table tennis equipment.

I have been privileged to have a private viewing of Rex Haggett's unique collection of table tennis postcards and he has been most helpful with advice on the early history of the game.

Tom King drew the diagram on page 4 with meticulous care.

Photographs and other illustrations are acknowledged as follows: the British Broadcasting Corporation, page 16 (top); Tony Ellis, page 9; the Wimbledon Lawn Tennis Museum, pages 3, 17, 26, 28 (both), 29 (upper right and lower), 30 (top); Grandad's Photography Museum, all others.

COVER: *Detail from 'All about Our Lawn Tennis Club', drawn by Arthur Hopkins for 'The Graphic', summer number, 1886.*

BELOW: *Very rare and immaculate ping-pong battledores with single vellum sheet held in varnished bamboo frames; 18 inches (460 mm) overall; patented by J. R. Mally in 1901.*

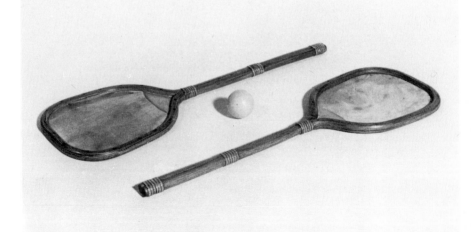

A delightful late nineteenth-century painting of domestic lawn tennis.

INTRODUCTION

Interest in the paraphernalia of early games is steadily increasing. The opening in 1977 of the Wimbledon Lawn Tennis Museum at the All England Club created interest in both the history and the equipment of lawn tennis, although many items in the museum, even if they could be found, would be well beyond the pocket of the ordinary collector.

Even the long-standing manufacturers of rackets and other equipment do not necessarily have items from the distant past, and the national associations of badminton, table tennis and squash have ephemera only and little or no equipment.

Diligent searching is needed but many interesting and aesthetically pleasing items are still to be found in second-hand shops and at antiques fairs. Rackets are often underpriced since dealers are commonly ignorant of the differences between a 'granny' racket of the 1930s and an antique or 'early' racket from the 1880s. Some racketana is included from time to time in Phillips' sales of sporting items but these tend to be dominated by cricket and golf.

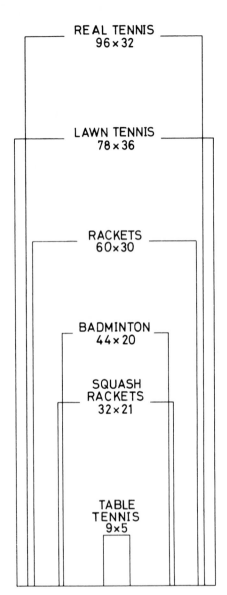

REAL TENNIS
96 × 32

LAWN TENNIS
78 × 36

RACKETS
60 × 30

BADMINTON
44 × 20

SQUASH
RACKETS
32 × 21

TABLE
TENNIS
9 × 5

GLOSSARY

Badminton: the relatively modern sport played with a racket and shuttlecock; a formalised version of battledore and shuttlecock.

Battledore and shuttlecock: a garden game superseded by badminton and long extinct.

Lawn tennis: known popularly as tennis. The outdoor version of real tennis, first played on a lawn and later on various hard surfaces.

Rackets: a rare indoor game, played mainly in Britain, which involves hitting a hard ball within four walls.

Real tennis: the early 'sport of kings', from which all racket games descend, and now very rare. Sometimes known as royal tennis.

Squash rackets: known popularly as squash and played very extensively. Similar to rackets but played in a smaller court and with a soft, 'squashy' ball.

Table tennis: a miniaturised indoor version of lawn tennis, known in its early days by various trade names including Table Tennis, Gossima, Ping Pong, Parlour Tennis, Whiff-Waff and Indoor Tennis. The implement used is properly known as a 'racket', not a 'bat' as commonly supposed.

LEFT: *Court dimensions. This diagram shows the court dimensions, the actual playing areas of the various games (in feet). A real tennis court is not precisely rectangular but approximates to the size shown. The total recommended playing area for lawn tennis is 120 feet by 60 feet (36.6 m by 18.3 m); for badminton it is 52 feet by 28 feet (15.8 m by 8.5 m) and for table tennis 46 feet by 23 feet (14.0 m by 7.0 m).*

The Reverend J. T. Hartley beating H. F. Lawford in the 1880 Wimbledon final. From the 'Illustrated London News'.

THE ORIGINS OF RACKET GAMES

Although certain family likenesses can be discerned between all racket games, no distinct genealogical tree can be drawn to show their relationships. There are, however, three reasonably clear lines of descent: lawn tennis and table tennis are both descendants of real tennis; badminton is the offspring of battledore and shuttlecock; squash rackets is the direct descendant of rackets.

REAL TENNIS

Real tennis is the ancestor of all racket games and originated in France about a thousand years ago. 'Real' is an old form of 'royal' and the game is still sometimes known as royal tennis, indicating a long royal connection from Louis X of France in the fourteenth century to Henry VIII of England in the sixteenth. In its primitive form the game was played with the hand and in France it is still known as *le jeu de paume*. It was probably around 1500 that the racket was introduced. Sometime in the fourteenth century the game was imported to England but the

oldest surviving court still in use today, that at Hampton Court Palace, was not built until 1530. There are about a dozen others in various parts of Britain.

The court used in real tennis is a far more elaborate structure than a rackets or squash rackets court and was originally modelled on the cloisters of French monasteries, where the game proved such a distraction from monastic affairs that it was often banned by the church authorities. In simple terms it is rather as if a squash court were quadrupled in size and then had added to it a few apertures in the walls and some sloping shelves as well as a net.

The court is a very expensive structure and real tennis will never be a popular game, but its place in the history of racket games and the mystique and grandeur it evokes ensure that it will remain 'the sport of kings and king of sports'.

LAWN TENNIS

Lawn tennis is a direct descendant of real tennis or, more accurately, an

LEFT: *A woodburytype of C. W. Grinstead, 'the model of imperturbability', who had a brief but distinguished career before emigrating in 1885. He partnered C. E. Welldon to win the Wimbledon doubles in 1883.*

RIGHT: *Miss L. Dod, Wimbledon champion on five occasions before (in the words of a contemporary writer) she 'defected to golf'.*

adaptation of real tennis for the social needs of the 1870s. Credit for this is commonly given to Major Walter Clopton Wingfield, a retired army officer and gentleman farmer in Wales, for he had the business sense to see that the time was ripe for a 'new' game. Many people observed that it was not new at all and his application to the patents office in 1874 never gave him more than provisional protection.

There were several earlier experiments with simplified versions of real tennis on a lawn; half a dozen were listed by C. G. Heathcote in his contribution to the Badminton Library series, 1890. In particular, insufficient credit has probably been given to Harry Gem, a Birmingham solicitor, who in 1865 set up a game of 'lawn rackets' in his garden at 8 Ampton Road, Edgbaston. The lawn still survives, but severely obstructed by an air-raid shelter, a relic of the Second World War. In 1872 Gem and a Spanish friend, Augurio Perera, set up the first lawn tennis club at Leamington Spa, where Gem died in 1881.

Major Wingfield was an entrepreneur rather than an inventor but he did much to popularise the game and he was shrewd enough to admit his early mistakes; he soon agreed to abandon the absurd title 'sphairistiké', which he had contrived for his game, for the more practical (and more easily pronounced) 'lawn tennis'. He also accepted the rectangular rather than the 'hour-glass' court, 30 feet (9.1 m) at the baseline and 21 feet (6.4 m) at the net, which appeared in the specifications for his patent application and survived for only a short period.

When, in 1875, the All England Croquet Club introduced lawn tennis to its lawns, the future of the game was assured though the rules were not settled (very much in their present form) until the first Wimbledon Championships in 1877. These championships now attract the world's top players from nearly fifty countries.

TABLE TENNIS

The Victorians were very fond of what

we now call miniaturisation and many outdoor games, including cricket, croquet, bowls, golf and lawn tennis, were reduced to indoor versions. Of these only table tennis has survived, becoming a major sport in its own right.

Table tennis is like so many games in that no precise date can be cited for its invention. For many years it has been said that the earliest advertisement appeared in 1884 when F. H. Ayres Limited offered their 'Miniature Indoor Lawn Tennis Game' to the public. But no copy of this advertisement can now be traced and it remains open to question whether this was a version of table tennis. Lawn tennis was already well established and the table version was, at some stage, an almost inevitable offspring; it seems certain, particularly as the equipment was so easily improvised, that many households devised their own games for long winter evenings in the 1870s, but no positive evidence of this has yet emerged. The dining table was still an essential in every home and a net was easily improvised with a piece of string stretched between two strategically placed chairs or even champagne bottles. A crudely shaped piece of cardboard or wood made an adequate racket or the old battledore could be pressed into service.

Initially the lack of a suitable ball

proved a serious drawback to the development of the game; cork was tried but did not give enough bounce and a rubber ball proved too lively. But in the early 1890s James Gibb, a Surrey engineer and noted athlete, suggested to his neighbour John Jaques, a sports manufacturer, that he should produce a celluloid ball for the game. Jaques took up this idea and patented his own version of the game, under the title 'Gossima', in 1891.

There is a much repeated story that James Gibb invented the name 'ping-pong' on hearing the sound of the ball on racket and table, but evidence in the form of a dated ping-pong greetings card suggests that the name dates from at least 1878.

Table tennis enjoyed a spectacular boom around 1900, primarily as a postprandial parlour game for the genteel, but it was a craze which quickly passed and the game faded almost into oblivion for a period of fifteen years. It was not until 1922 that the game was revived by three enthusiasts including Percy Bromfield, who had been English champion since 1904. The English Table Tennis Association was set up in 1926 and established firm rules. International competition soon followed; there are now over 120 countries in membership of the International Table Tennis Federation.

Ping-pong on the dining table. This illustration is one of several in the 'Royal Magazine' in 1901.

LEFT: *An illustration of battledore and shuttlecock by Kate Greenaway (1846-1901) for one of her children's books. She often showed children in dress of an earlier period.*
RIGHT: *Charles Read, in typical dress of the period, demonstrates an 'angle stroke to left side-wall' in his book 'Squash Rackets', 1929. In the 1920s he was professional champion of the British Isles in squash rackets, rackets and lawn tennis.*

BADMINTON

The use of a shuttlecock rather than a ball — although in the early days balls (stuffed with feathers) were sometimes used — makes badminton no closer than a cousin to the other racket games.

Badminton is descended directly from the ancient game of battledore and shuttlecock. This was primarily a children's game but nineteenth-century illustrations often show adults playing, mostly in the garden but sometimes indoors. Battledore and shuttlecock was never more than a genial and gentle recreation and was not even competitive, the idea being for the players to co-operate in keeping the shuttlecock in the air for as long as possible and counting the number of hits. The story runs that it was at Badminton House, the seat of the Dukes of Beaufort, in the middle of the nineteenth century, that a net — in the form of a piece of string — was first introduced so that the players took opposing sides. This may well have been the beginning of the modern sport of badminton, but no written contemporary record survives and there is a rival claim that badminton was first played by the British in India and then imported into Britain, about 1874, by returning army officers. It may well be that the game was then taken up and popularised at Badminton House, which at the very least provided a lasting name.

Although badminton had the advantage that a relatively small (and not necessarily level) lawn was needed, it did not catch the public imagination in the same way as lawn tennis; it was slow to develop as a serious sport. Early attempts to establish firm rules had been made at Poona in the 1870s, but no standard version was universally accepted until the newly formed Badminton Association set to work in 1893. Badminton is now played worldwide in fifty-eight countries.

RACKETS

Rackets and squash rackets, both of which utilise walls but no net, together make a third family of racket games,

8

relating in certain respects to pelota, the ancient Spanish and French game, rather than to the English-bred 'tennis' games.

Early forms of rackets were played in an informal manner against any convenient wall, with drainpipes or buttresses being regarded as interesting hazards. It is clear from Charles Dickens's account of rackets at the Fleet Prison in *Pickwick Papers* (1836) that the court at that time had only two sides. There is no evidence that Dickens ever visited the Fleet but a painting by Thomas Rowlandson (1807) shows a remarkably similar scene. If it were not for Dickens and Rowlandson the Fleet would not figure so strongly in the various histories of the game; it is open to question whether the Fleet was really (as so often claimed) the birthplace of rackets rather than merely one of the places where the game was played.

The all-important transition to a closed, covered court took place in the 1850s when the Prince's Club, Knightsbridge, was opened; the nature and technique of the game changed dramatically. The Prince's Club played a predominant role in the game until the Queen's Club, West Kensington, opened in 1887. This is still the primary centre for the game, which is otherwise almost entirely restricted to the public schools and older universities.

SQUASH RACKETS

No two racket games are more closely related than rackets and squash rackets; all authorities seem to agree that squash rackets originated, probably in the mid nineteenth century, at Harrow School among boys waiting to play rackets. Somerville Gibney, an old Harrovian, in a little-known article in *The Boy's Own Paper*, June 1894, says: 'Give a Harrow boy a wall — if a blank one so much the better — and two others, or even one other, at right angles to it, with a clear space between, and the probability is that it won't be long before he is busy at squash rackets.' But he goes on to say

A 1980s reconstruction in an Essex garden of Victorian battledore and shuttlecock, probably only the second time the game has been played since 1900.

that the more formal version of squash had its origin in the Rugby fives courts at Harrow; this has a ring of probability about it. In the smaller space a soft 'squashy' ball was essential to slow down the game, and it is believed that this is how the name originated.

The area of a squash court is only about two-fifths that of a rackets court and the expense of the latter caused it to be gradually superseded by the newer game. Squash developed steadily through the public schools and in the 1920s and 1930s became very popular with the British forces, who took the game with them overseas. Furthermore squash flourished at many West End clubs, and over the years purpose-built clubs sprang up all over Britain; in the early 1980s over fifteen hundred clubs were registered with the Squash Rackets Association, the governing body of the game.

RACKETS

The very earliest implement for striking a ball was, naturally, the hand itself; there is clear evidence for this in illustrations from as early as the fourteenth century. Racket makers still strive continually to perfect a racket, whether for lawn tennis, badminton or squash, which provides, as far as possible, a natural extension of the hand and arm so as to achieve the maximum control and power with the minimum effort.

Nearly all the rackets which survive from the Victorian and Edwardian periods are of fine quality and workmanship, and it is clear that the racket makers took considerable pride in their craft. In 1908 Grays of Cambridge employed two men on racket production, together making about two dozen rackets per week, entirely by hand; perhaps in this context the word should be 'racquets' for Grays is the only company which still retains the old spelling. Many of the rackets made during this period would be perfectly serviceable today.

Lawn tennis rackets are chunky and solid, often with a rich patina of contrasting woods; badminton rackets are fragile by comparison, their very lightness making for a delicate quality.

Early rackets — up to about 1930 — were steam-bent; a 'stick' of rendered ash was subjected to steam at a very high temperature and, when sufficiently pliable, fixed round a form so as to give the desired shape of head, whether flat-topped, round, oval or lop-sided. Since the 1930s rackets have been laminated, that is the frame is made up in layers of different woods which are bonded together. This method of construction makes the racket much stronger and avoids the risk of the frame splitting during manufacture.

For many years the handle was left completely uncovered, but it was often octagonally shaped to avoid risk of the player's hand slipping and might (for the same purpose) end with a 'fish-tail' or 'dolphin' butt, giving a very comfortable grip. It is surprising that this feature is no longer found. Some rackets have grooves along the handle to aid ventilation, notably Lunn's 'Patent Ventilated Holdfast Racket', but only at extra cost.

Catgut strings have nothing to do with cats. 'Cat' is a corruption of 'kit', a seventeenth-century violin. Natural gut strings are produced from the muscle tissue of the intestines of sheep; it takes the intestines of seven sheep to provide enough gut for one lawn tennis racket. In the mid sixteenth century the gut used in rackets was merely adapted from 'music-al' strings, but in 1870 Mr Bussey, the most notable racket manufacturer of the day, devised specifications for lawn tennis gut. These laid down the standard which is still in use today. Synthetic strings also date from the nineteenth century and as early as the 1920s experiments were made with steel strings (in aluminium frames) and later with silk, which proved too expensive. Modern synthetic strings followed the development of nylon in the early 1940s.

Various fancy methods of stringing rackets have been tried over the years; some rackets were strung diagonally and others (particularly very early ones) were strung with the gut laboriously knotted at each juncture. Many lawn tennis rackets from the early part of the twentieth century have longitudinal double mains — extra strings down the centre designed to give extra strength where it is needed most. But these methods have long been abandoned in favour of the pattern of stringing which is familiar in modern rackets.

ABOVE: *(From left) Very early racket (game unknown) with the cross strings turned each time they meet the mains. Real tennis racket, showing the lop-sided head. Squash rackets racket, 1900, slightly shorter than rackets racket. Battledore and shuttlecock racket, 1890s, unusually large; 23 inches (584 mm) overall.*

BELOW: *(From left) Lawn tennis racket, 1880, showing influence of real tennis. Modern rackets racket made by Grays. Badminton racket, 1880, with pear-shaped head. Ping-pong battledore, 1900.*

11

SLAZENGERS'
Sets of Lawn Tennis in Boxes.

No. 480—The "TRAVELLING" Set.

In well-made Box containing four "La Belle" Rackets, twelve uncovered Balls, Poles, Cords and Runners complete, Steam Tarred Net, Centre Guide, Brush and Chalk to mark out Courts, and Book of Rules and Instructions.

An early Slazengers' advertisement for their boxed lawn tennis set containing four 'La Belle' rackets. These sets are very rare.

Real tennis rackets retain their characteristic asymmetrical head which lawn tennis abandoned in its early days; this feature survives because the shape allows the player to retain the ball on the racket for the maximum time and achieve an effective 'slice'. The ball used in real tennis is solid and relatively hard, and the racket is therefore strung with a very heavy-gauge gut, which traditionally is always black. Because of the esoteric nature of the game very few early real tennis rackets are to be found.

The basic design of lawn tennis rackets

Fine 'La Belle' lawn tennis racket dating from about 1900 and with its original strings almost intact.

has hardly changed at all, even over a period of nearly a hundred years; rackets today, as in the 1880s, are about 27 inches (686 mm) long and weigh (according to the taste of the player) around 13 or 14 ounces (370 - 400 g). The shape of the head, however, has gone through various fashions, with a steady transition from the rather flat-topped head to the oval or rounded one. A convex wedge, often of a darker wood, is a feature of most rackets up to about 1905 and this can still be found even in the 1920s. Fashions tended to overlap, with some manufacturers continuing with features long abandoned by others. Even the experts in this field are therefore very careful in the dating of rackets.

Lawn tennis is unique among racket games in showing a liking for gadgetry; there are early rackets with scoring mechanisms set into the handle and others with means of varying the tension of the strings. The most comprehensive collections are to be found at the Wimbledon Lawn Tennis Museum and at Bow Brand Limited. Both these collections include rackets which display the latest

BELOW: *A very well preserved 1920s lawn tennis racket with 'fish-tail' grip and double mains for additional strength in the centre of the racket.*
BOTTOM: *Child's racket only 23 inches (584 mm) long and dating from about 1890. It may be intended for lawn tennis or for use with a shuttlecock.*

technology in design and manufacture such as the Dunlop Max 200G injection-moulded fibre racket.

In the mid nineteenth century there were only two racket makers in England, T. H. Prosser and Sons, of Pentonville, and Nusser, but with the invention of lawn tennis an enormous number of small firms came into existence in the last quarter of the century, even if only as subsidiaries to the large companies such as Slazenger, Ayres and Bussey. Unfortunately, rackets often do not show the manufacturer's name.

The most famous individual racket maker of this period was Thomas Tate, foreman to Buchanan of Piccadilly. He was so much in demand by leading players for rackets made to their own design that he could charge them twice the normal cost. Rackets at this time were advertised at £1. Having established a market in one sport, manufacturers tended to extend their range and the same well known names appear in various games. The Renshaw twins, William and Ernest, who dominated the top championships in the 1880s, were endorsing rackets (and lawn tennis shoes) as early as 1885. Reggie Doherty followed this up some years later when his own design of racket was sold with his 'autograph' in gilt.

Before the first manufactured table tennis sets were offered to the public in the 1880s, the rackets were crudely

ABOVE: *A highly decorated and very well finished 1930s lawn tennis racket shown alongside one from the 1880s. The convex wedge and squarer head of the latter are clear indications of age.*
BELOW: *Fine mahogany racket press with brass fittings. In 1895 these were sold by Harrod's Stores for 5s 9d.*

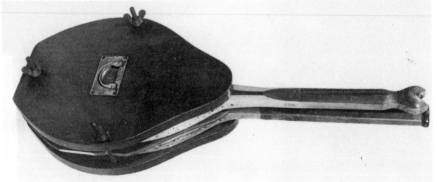

RIGHT: *Advertisements are a very good source of information on racket styles. This is from the 'Lawn Tennis Magazine', 1885.*

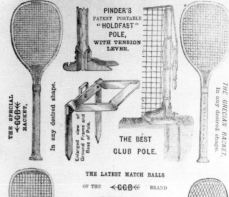

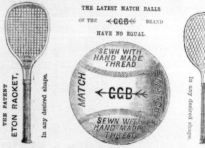

BELOW LEFT: *Photograph (18 inches by 9 inches, 460 mm by 230 mm) by H. Jetter, showing how even in the 1920s players did not readily keep their eye on the ball.*

BELOW RIGHT: *Mrs Hillyard, lady champion of England, in a striking portrait, 1900, displaying both the costume and the racket of the period.*

LEFT: *Actress Madeline Smith, using an early Jaques battledore, demonstrates a ladylike service during a reconstruction of an 1890s table tennis game for the BBC Television series 'Eureka' in 1983. A cork ball was used; champagne bottles served as posts and cigar-box lids as rackets.*

RIGHT: *An original and exceedingly rare sphairistiké set made in 1874 with rackets by Jefferies and Mallings.*

BELOW: *Victorian or Edwardian table tennis set with 'drum racquets'. Often (as here) the contents do not match up to the illustration.*

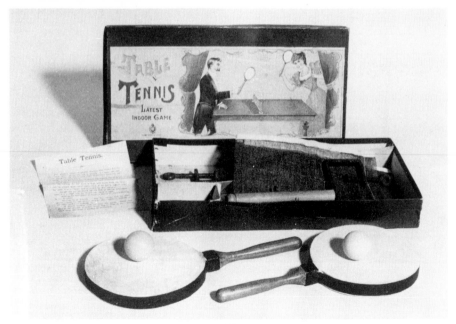

16

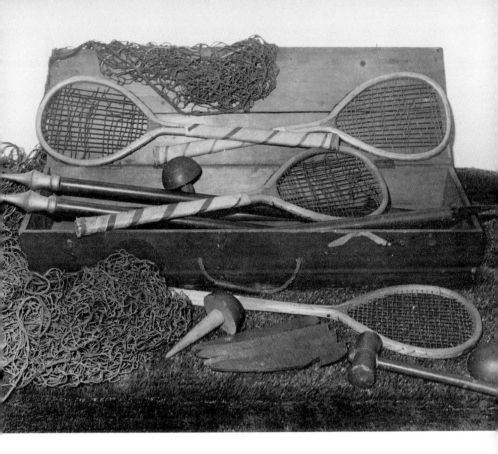

fashioned from cardboard or wood or adapted from the battledores used in the ancient game of battledore and shuttlecock; these are often found with the handles cut down for the parlour game. No doubt books were then (as now) pressed into service by schoolboys. Later rackets were constructed in a wide variety of materials including cork, plywood and solid mahogany. Various covering materials were used: sandpaper, pimpled rubber and, more recently, 'sponge' rubber. The early advertisements show that experiments were even made with gutstrung rackets on the model of lawn tennis, but these offer the player practically no control of the ball and were quickly abandoned. Not surprisingly, very few strung table tennis rackets have survived. Many of the rackets dating from the table tennis boom around 1900 to 1905 are of exquisite quality, with elegantly shaped blades and handles.

Jaques and Son, who had already been established for over a hundred years, sold enormous numbers of their 'Gossima' or 'Ping Pong' boxed sets in association with Hamley Brothers. They designed their own purpose-made battledore; this is most commonly 15 inches (381 mm) in length, compared to the 18 inches (457 mm) or more of the old battledore, and consists of a lightweight frame fixed to a wooden handle and covered on both sides with vellum. True vellum is sheepskin or calfskin dressed with chalk, a covering considered far superior to the cheaper parchment (merely paper treated with sulphuric acid). Imitations were produced and Jaques found it necessary to mark each battledore 'Warranted best vellum'. Their rackets are always finely decorated with gilt and (as a further mark of the quality of that time) one racket in a

ABOVE: *Ping Pong was the name registered by J. Jaques and Son, in 1900, for their very popular version of table tennis.*

BELOW: *There was fierce competition among manufacturers, and Grays of Cambridge produced their free-standing net in the 1890s with the claim that it avoided damage to the table edge. With it is one of a pair of elegantly shaped vellum battledores from a Jaques set.*

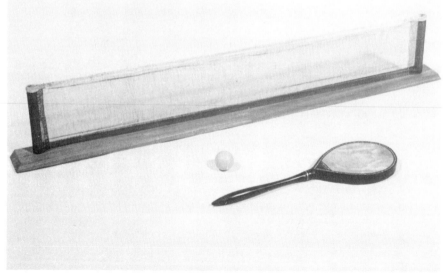

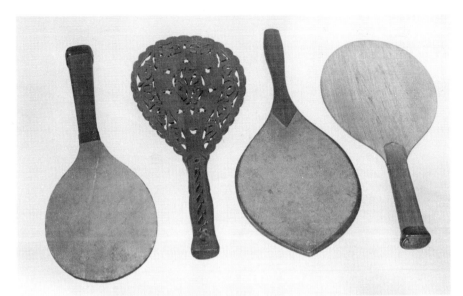

ABOVE: *Table tennis rackets were made in various shapes. These wooden rackets all date from about 1900 when the parlour game was at the height of its popularity. The fretwork racket is probably the only one in existence; it is known that it was home-made in 1905.*

BELOW: *Very rare strung table tennis rackets dating from the 1890s. The centre racket also has one vellum face, allowing the player to use either surface.*

pair has a thinner handle for the lady's more genteel hand.

The battledore played an important part in the development not only of table tennis but also of badminton. The history of the battledore is obscure but it is clear from an illustrated manuscript in the British Library that it dates back (at least in its wooden form) to the fourteenth century. Probably the earliest surviving vellum battledore is that in the West Highland Museum, Fort William. It is claimed that this belonged to John Cameron of Fassifern, who was born in 1771 and killed in action at Quatre Bras in 1815. This is identical in design to the battledore used for the family recreation of battledore and shuttlecock until the end of the nineteenth century, most notably at Badminton House, Avon,

LEFT: *Late nineteenth-century badminton racket, elegantly shaped and finely balanced.*

BELOW: *The All-England badminton champions of 1905, drawn by Ralph Cleaver for the 'Illustrated Sporting and Dramatic News': on the left, Dr H. N. Marrett, reputedly the first outstanding champion; on the right, Miss M. Lucas, who won through from a small entry. Doubles was much more popular among ladies at the time.*

Mᴿ H.N. Marrett
Winner
Gentlemen's Singles

Miss M. Lucas
Winner of
Ladies Singles

20

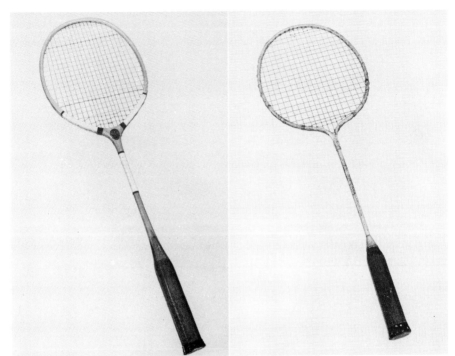

LEFT: *A 1930s 'Vitiv' badminton racket by Muller, of the Strand.*
RIGHT: *Unusual 1920s badminton racket with steel shaft and head and wire stringing; made by the Dayton Racquet Company, Ohio, USA.*

where some fine samples still survive, including one with a handwritten inscription dated 1830.

The battledore was superseded by the badminton racket when badminton evolved in the early 1860s. A nineteenth-century racket can be recognised by the pear-shaped head, the darkness of the wood and, perhaps, by identifying marks. Occasionally an Indian racket will be found with the name 'Sialkote' incised along the handle, thereby confirming the importance of India in the development of the game. Sialkote was an area of the Punjab annexed by the British after the Second Sikh War in 1849 and is still noted for the manufacture of sporting equipment.

Around 1900 rackets were by no means standardised and the same racket might well serve a dual purpose. Eustace H. Miles, in the first full-length (and very rare) book on squash, published in 1901, recommends lawn tennis players to use a shortened tennis racket for squash (or 'squash-tennis' as he calls it), although preferring a purpose-made racket rather shorter than the rackets racket then in use. He says that this could be obtained from either Slazenger or Prosser; the price at this time was only a few shillings for a racket made entirely by hand. Slazenger celebrated its first hundred years of sports manufacturing in 1981 but Prosser, founded in 1857, has long faded from the sporting scene. Squash rackets (and rackets rackets) have changed over the years even less than lawn tennis rackets, with virtually no alteration in size or shape. But the early rackets were very plain and unadorned. Not until the late 1920s or early 1930s did rackets appear with distinguishing features — a highly polished finish, coloured decorative bindings and fancy names, such as Wisden's 'College', Jameson's 'Zenith' and 'University'.

21

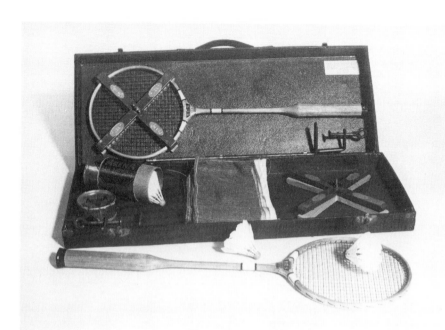

ABOVE: 'Arena Table Badminton' with miniature silk-strung rackets, 22 inches (559 mm) overall, and elegant shuttlecocks (2½ inches, 64 mm). This is a rare item from the 1930s and sold then for 45s. BELOW: A Grays evolution set showing some of the stages in the manufacture of a squash racket.

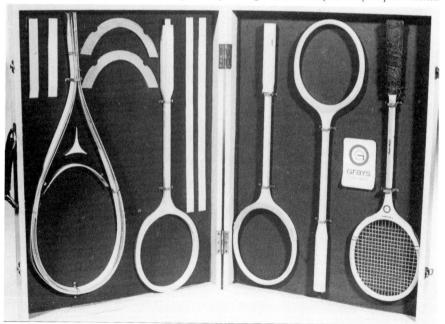

LEFT: *1920s lawn tennis balls 'pronounced by "The Field" Absolutely Perfect'. Although the box is distressed, the balls are in new, unused condition.*
RIGHT: *Very fine shuttlecock (one of a set of five) probably made in India about 1840. The feathers are 4 inches (100 mm) long and stuck into a cork base covered with kid leather and velvet, decorated with braid.*

BALLS AND SHUTTLECOCKS

All racket games by definition require some kind of projectile; this may take the form of a ball or a shuttlecock. Very often it was the invention of a more satisfactory projectile which brought an important step forward in the development of a game.

The table tennis boom in the 1890s came directly from James Gibb's improvised use of a xylonite toy ball which he had found when on a business trip to America. Sometimes this was even covered with a hand-sewn cloth but this experiment was soon abandoned and such balls are now very rare.

The development of lawn tennis depended greatly on the discovery of a ball which would give a satisfactory bounce on a grass surface. Early rubber balls proved a major advance on the leather-covered ball, hand-made and stuffed with cloth, borrowed from real tennis. The cloth cover came later, giving a ball which was easier to control and much more durable. Until the late 1920s the seams were joined by stitching but it was then found that rubber cement gave a more satisfactory bond. The shape of the seam ensures that tennis balls (unlike cricket balls) take a true flight. There are about a dozen stages in the manufacture of a modern lawn tennis ball and it seems that this process can never be fully automated. In 1982 over 225 million balls were sold throughout the world.

The shuttlecock may have originated from the habit of storing quill feathers in a cork on the writing desk; perhaps one day in the eighteenth century such a pen-holder fell to the floor and its owner, noticing its flight, had discovered the shuttlecock. Certainly for many years shuttlecocks have been made with a cork base and with goose or chicken feathers carefully arranged so as to give a true flight. Nineteenth-century shuttlecocks were often much larger and heavier than modern ones, indicating that they were used for badminton in the garden or for battledore and shuttlecock.

These 1936 cigarette cards show famous players demonstrating the various lawn tennis strokes.

CIGARETTE CARDS

Lawn tennis is the only racket sport which has its own complete sets of cigarette or other trade cards; there are at least ten of these, the earliest of which is possibly the set of twenty-five cards issued by Nicholas Sarony and Company in 1923 under the title 'Tennis Strokes'.

This set was reissued by Cope Brothers in 1924 and five more cards were added in 1925. But it seems very likely that there were earlier cards around 1900.

1928 was a good year for lawn tennis cards with several issues: 'Lawn Tennis' (fifty plus twelve large-size cards) by W.

Gallaher cigarette cards (1928) showing (from the left) the British players D. M. Greig, O. G. N. Turnbull and Miss Joan Ridley.

24

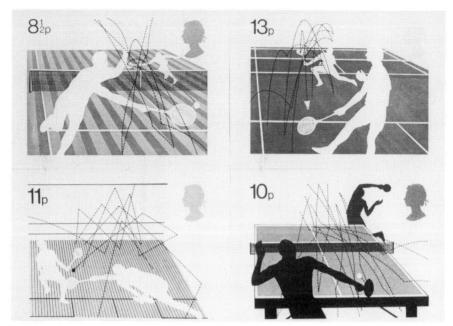

Four British stamps issued in 1977 to commemorate the racket sports lawn tennis, badminton, squash rackets and table tennis.

A. and A. C. Churchman; 'Lawn Tennis Celebrities' (fifty) by Gallaher Limited; 'Lawn Tennis' (fifty) published overseas by John Player and Son. Not surprisingly, this last set is rare.

In 1930 Godfrey Phillips produced 'Lawn Tennis' (twenty-five cards) and a year later W. D. and H. O. Wills followed this up with their set of twenty-five large-size cards under the same title. The most commonly found set, 'Tennis' (fifty) by John Player is often encountered in an album. Finally, in 1938, the Ardath Tobacco Company published their 'Tennis' (fifty).

Other racket sports are represented only by the odd card in a mixed set under such general titles as 'Sports and Games', 'Sports Champions' and 'Who's Who in Sport'. Nobody seems yet to have thought of publishing a set of cigarette cards under the title 'Racket Games'.

Cigarette cards are now taken more seriously by the auction houses, and many sets (or odd cards) are available to cartophiles from specialist dealers such as Murray Cards, Hendon.

POSTAGE STAMPS

The Post Office acknowledges that the most popular racket sports played in Britain today are lawn tennis, table tennis, squash and badminton (not necessarily in that order) and these are the sports — most notably lawn tennis and table tennis — which have supplied the subject for a large number of postage stamps. The idea has been taken up by a wide range of other countries wherever major sporting events are staged. As a result, this is a rich area for collectors, whether specialising in racket sports or a particular game. World championship events may well have their own postmarks to commemorate the occasion and these also are thoroughly collectable.

POSTCARDS AND PHOTOGRAPHS

Among racket sports only table tennis and lawn tennis have achieved the popularity which leads to the publication of picture postcards in quantity. These are highly collectable and in great demand. A private collector of table tennis cards has found over eighty such cards, the great majority of which date from the period 1902-5. This is towards the end of the era recognised by deltiologists as the heyday of picture postcards, both for quantity and quality, and it coincides with the remarkable boom in table tennis as a parlour game. Many of the cards are invitations to ping-pong parties with delightful coloured illustrations and simulated handwritten messages to be completed by the sender, for example: 'Do come along on . . . . night at . . . . o'clock to Ping Pong, expect a spirited game, Yours . . . .' Artists include Gordon Browne, Lance Thackeray, M. H. Tyler, F. H. Price and Louis Wain.

Lawn tennis cards are found more easily and are usually of the comic variety with a jocular play on words, for example 'love all'. Photographs may well show a court with players in action or a well known player with his 'autograph' superimposed. The more interesting picture postcards and photographs are most likely to be found at one of the large specialist fairs such as those held from time to time in South Kensington or at Cheltenham.

SILVERWARE AND CERAMICS

Among racket games it is practically only lawn tennis which has inspired the artist working in silver, ceramics or bronze. This might seem surprising, since all the racket games were thriving during the prolific Victorian and Edwardian ages, but only lawn tennis established its own strong social milieu. Tennis on the lawn soon led to tea on the lawn and inevitably to such items as tea services decorated with tennis scenes and silver teaspoons with racket-shaped handles. Several of the contemporary illustrations almost suggest that the game is secondary to the social chitchat and refreshments.

It is often not realised today that lawn

Silver brass tea gong in the elaborate Victorian manner and incorporating rackets, net and ball.

tennis stars such as the Renshaws and Dohertys were followed and idolised in the 1880s and 1890s. Any bronze figures such as that of one of the Doherty twins in the Wimbledon Lawn Tennis Museum must have been eagerly sought. In contrast with lawn tennis, the early champions of other racket games are usually little more than names.

Two 'write away' postcards drawn by Lance Thackeray. Two sets of these (each of six cards) were published by Raphael Tuck in 1902. The top card shows a net fitted with 'wings' to prevent the ball being returned round the net.

ABOVE: *Late nineteenth-century parian ware figures, 8 inches (200 mm) high. These show well the dress of players during this period.*

BELOW: *Victorian silver-plated inkstand incorporating lawn tennis items and dating from the 1880s.*

ABOVE RIGHT: *Tinted parian ware figure, 17½ inches (445 mm) high, modelled by James Morris about 1884, and possibly representing William Renshaw, Wimbledon champion for six years from 1881.*

ABOVE LEFT: *An unusual Victorian spelter figure showing a lady with racket and shuttlecock.*

RIGHT: *Rare Staffordshire pottery mug with blue transfer-printed lawn tennis scene of about 1885. Similar mugs showing football and cricket scenes are more common.*

LEFT: *Small, late nineteenth-century items of jewellery displayed in the Wimbledon Lawn Tennis Museum, some in sterling silver and others in soft metal.*

BELOW: *A parlour version of lawn tennis, with bone 'rackets' and 'balls', made in Germany. A cheaper version was produced in Britain in the 1930s.*

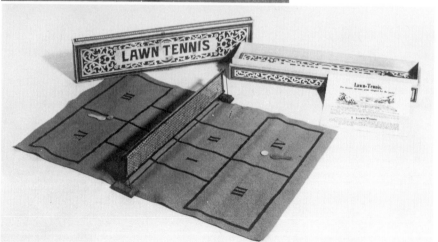

FURTHER READING

This is a small selection of books with useful information on the history and equipment of racket games. Playing manuals are omitted. An asterisk (*) indicates that the book is collectable in its own right.

GENERAL

Arlott, J. (editor). *Oxford Companion to Sports and Games.* Oxford University Press, 1975.
*Bolton, F. (editor). *Every Boy's Book of Sport and Pastime.* Routledge, 1905.
Cunnington, P., and Mansfield, A. *English Costume for Sports and Outdoor Recreation.* A. and C. Black, 1969.
Jewell, B. *Sports and Games.* Midas Books, 1976.
Viney, N., and Grant, N. *An Illustrated History of Ball Games.* Heinemann, 1978.
Complete Book of Sports and Pastimes. Cassell, 1896.

LAWN TENNIS

Clerici, G. *Tennis.* Octopus Books, 1976.
*Heathcote, J. M. (editor). *Tennis, Lawn Tennis, Rackets, Fives* (Badminton Library). Longmans, Green and Company, 1901.
*Myers, A. W. *Lawn Tennis at Home and Abroad.* Newnes, 1903.
*Myers, A. W. *Lawn Tennis: Its Principles and Practice.* Seeley and Company, 1930. (Contains an unusual section on rackets and balls.)
Warren, V. *The Wimbledon Lawn Tennis Museum.* 1982. (A history of lawn tennis as well as a guide to the Museum.)
The Kenneth Ritchie Wimbledon Library. 1982. (A catalogue of virtually all lawn tennis books written in English as well as many foreign ones.)

SQUASH RACKETS

Horry, J. *History of Squash Rackets.* A. C. M. Webb, 1979.
*Miles, E. H. *The Game of Squash.* Bell, 1901.

BADMINTON

Adams, B. *The Badminton Story.* BBC Publications, 1980.

TABLE TENNIS

*Parker, A. *Ping Pong and How to Play It.* Unwin, 1900. (The first book on the game; contains a very useful section on rackets.)

31

PLACES TO VISIT

Some sporting items are to be found at the *Victoria and Albert Museum* (Cromwell Road, South Kensington, London SW7 2RL; telephone 01-589 6371) and the *Museum of London* (London Wall, London EC2Y 5HN; telephone 01-600 3699) but there are very few specialised museums.

By far the most comprehensive collection of lawn tennis miscellanea is to be found at the *Wimbledon Lawn Tennis Museum,* The All England Club, Church Road, Wimbledon, London SW19 5AE; telephone 01-946 6131). The museum tells the story of lawn tennis and related games, with sections devoted to all the racket games. The museum is normally open each day from Tuesday to Sunday but is closed on Mondays. So that extensive alterations may be carried out, the museum will be closed from the end of the 1984 championships for about one year. It is wise to telephone the museum to check on opening times before paying a visit.

Incorporated in the museum is the Kenneth Ritchie Wimbledon Library, comprising a comprehensive range of books and ephemera. Application for a reader's pass should be made to the museum.

The widest collection of rackets covering all racket games is to be found at *Bow Brand Limited,* 2-3 Charterhouse Square, London EC1M 6ES, where there is also a small library. Intending visitors should apply in writing for an appointment.

Grays of Cambridge, Playfair Works, Benson Street, Cambridge, has a small but interesting collection of early rackets made by the company. Viewing is by prior appointment only.

A few items are on permanent loan to the *Cambridge and County Folk Museum* nearby at 2/3 Castle Street, Cambridge CB3 0AQ; telephone Cambridge (0223) 355159.

Collectors and serious researchers will be very welcome to see the *Gurney Collection of Early Table Tennis Equipment;* this is claimed to be by far the largest in the world. An appointment is necessary; telephone Colchester (0206) 230330.

Readers in the United States should visit *Texas Tennis Museum and Hall of Fame,* L401 Jefferson, Waco, Texas, and the *International Tennis Hall of Fame and Tennis Museum,* 194 Bellevue Avenue, Newport, Rhode Island 02840.

Miscellaneous lawn tennis items: a finely turned ball cleaner, an unusual racket press, Grays 'Gut Preserver' and a tape measure for marking out courts.